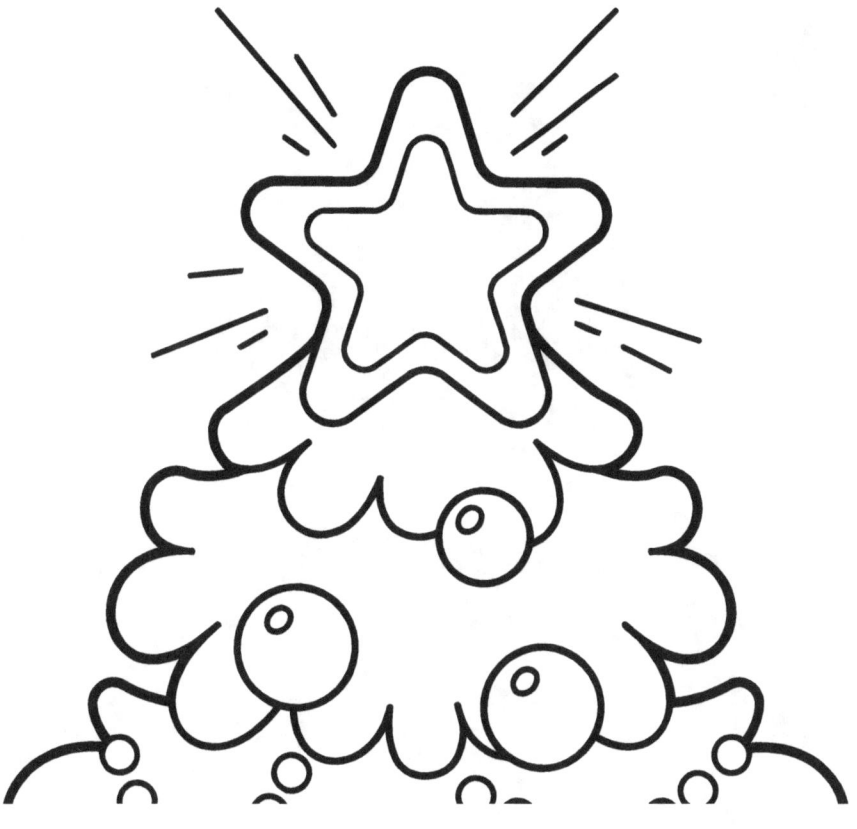

This Book Belongs To:

_____

_____

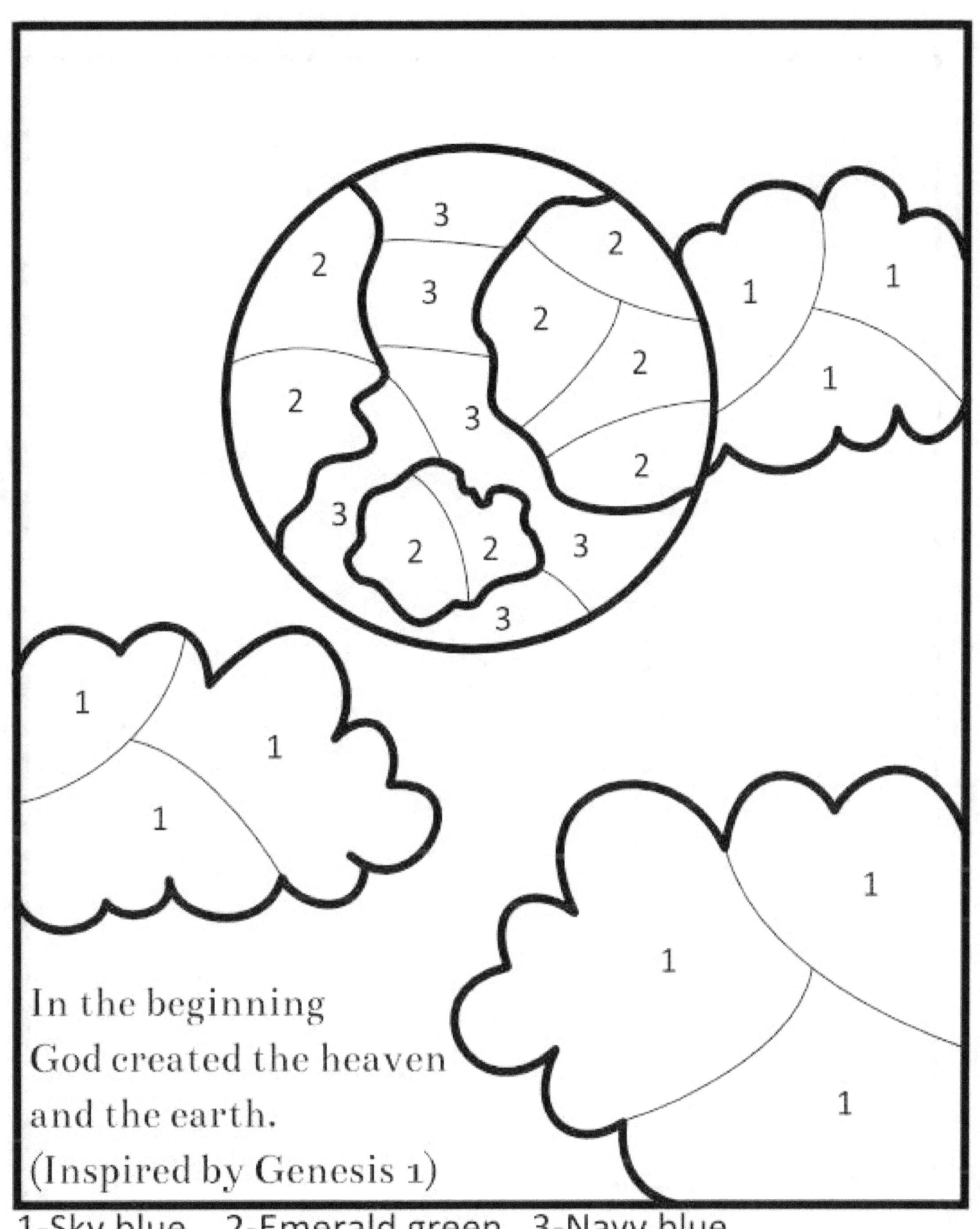

In the beginning
God created the heaven
and the earth.
(Inspired by Genesis 1)

1-Sky blue   2-Emerald green   3-Navy blue

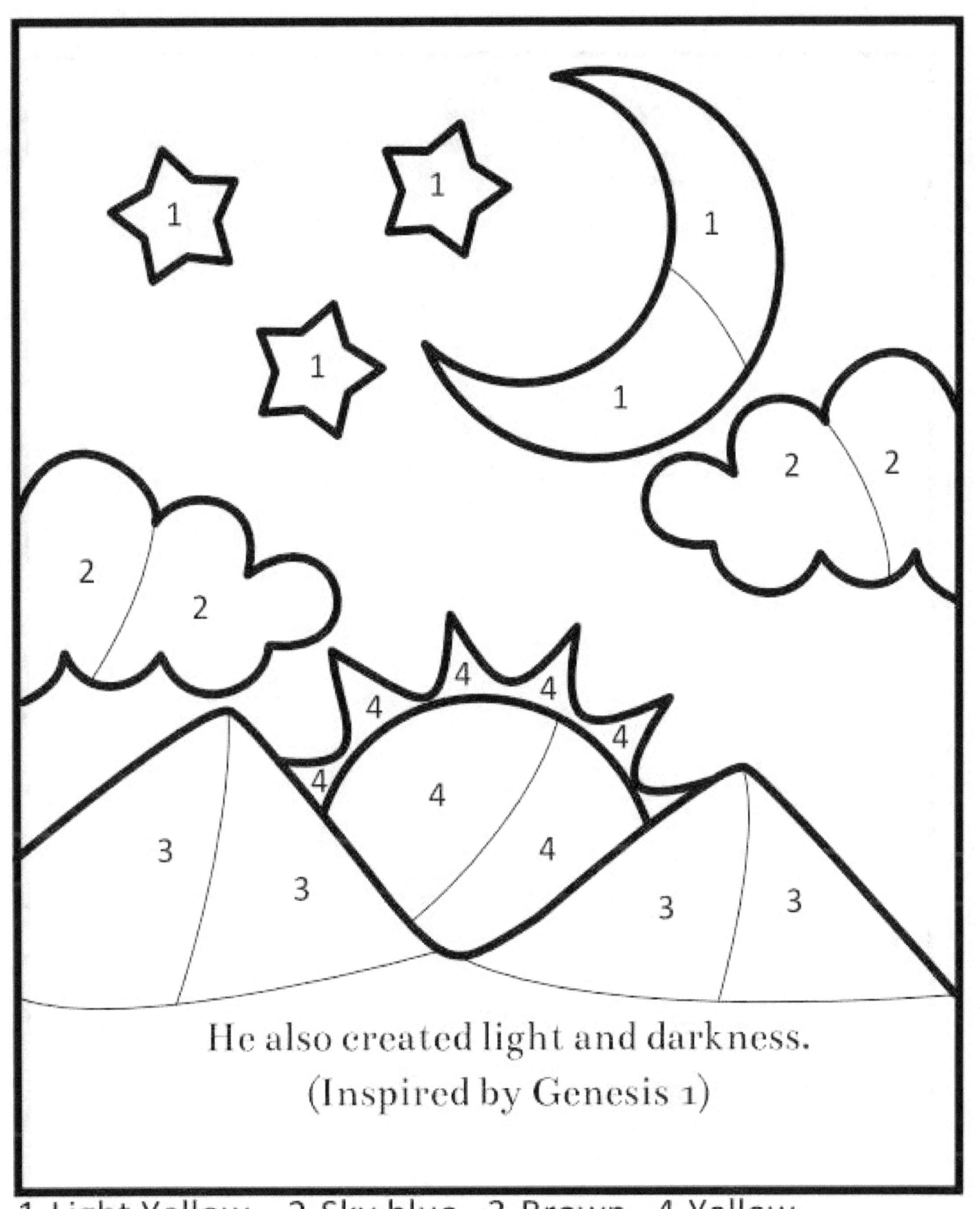

He also created light and darkness.
(Inspired by Genesis 1)

1-Light Yellow   2-Sky blue   3-Brown   4-Yellow

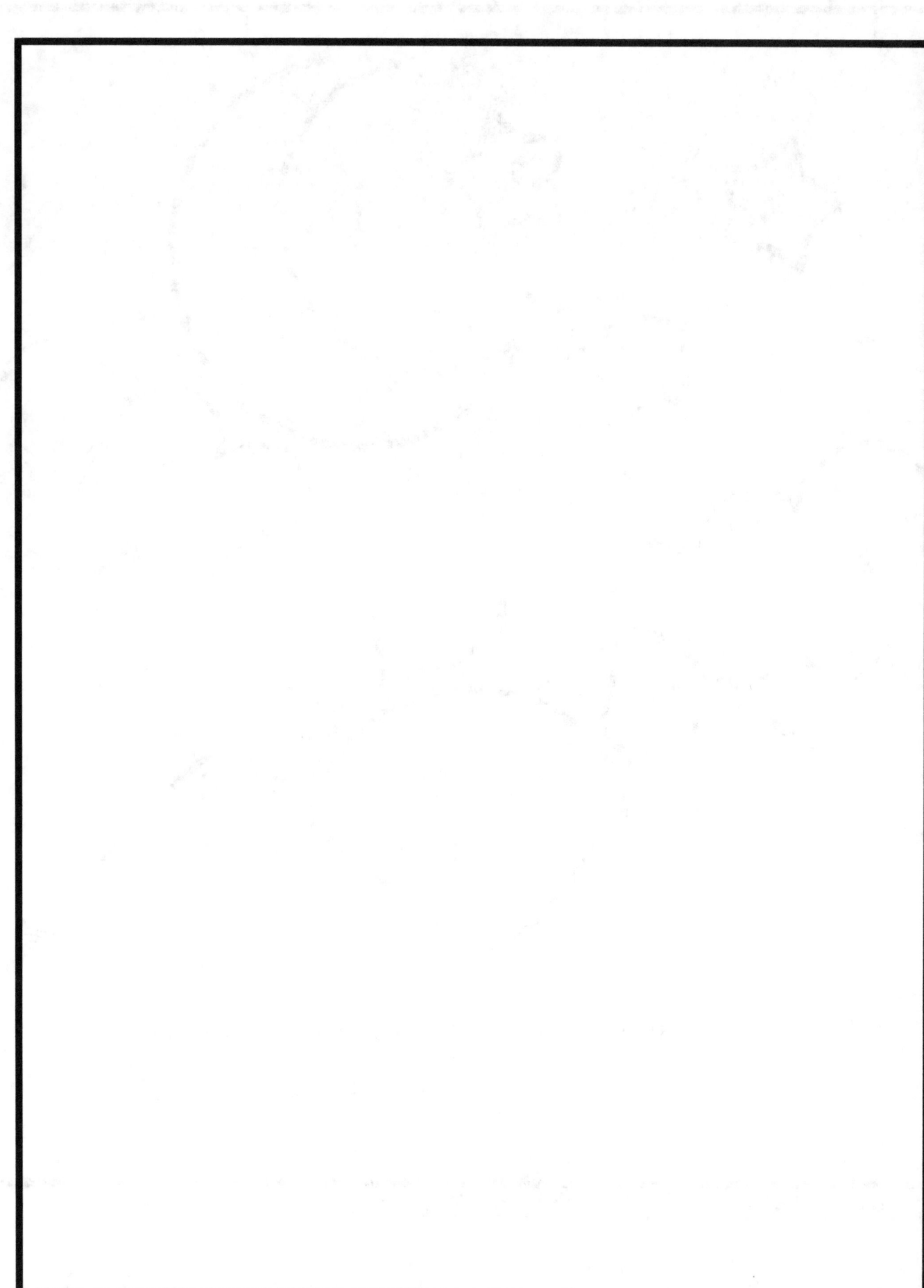

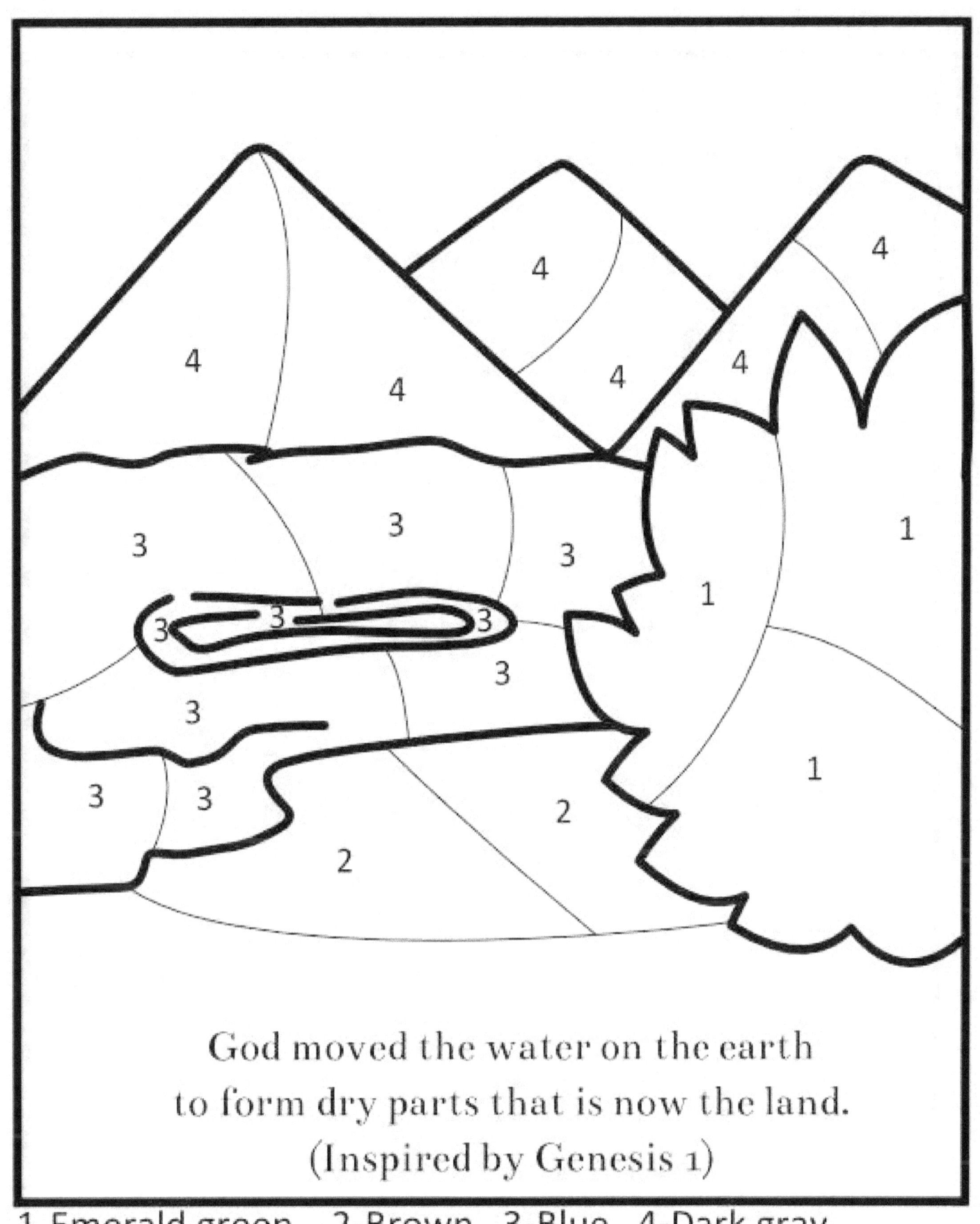

God moved the water on the earth
to form dry parts that is now the land.
(Inspired by Genesis 1)

1-Emerald green   2-Brown   3-Blue   4-Dark gray

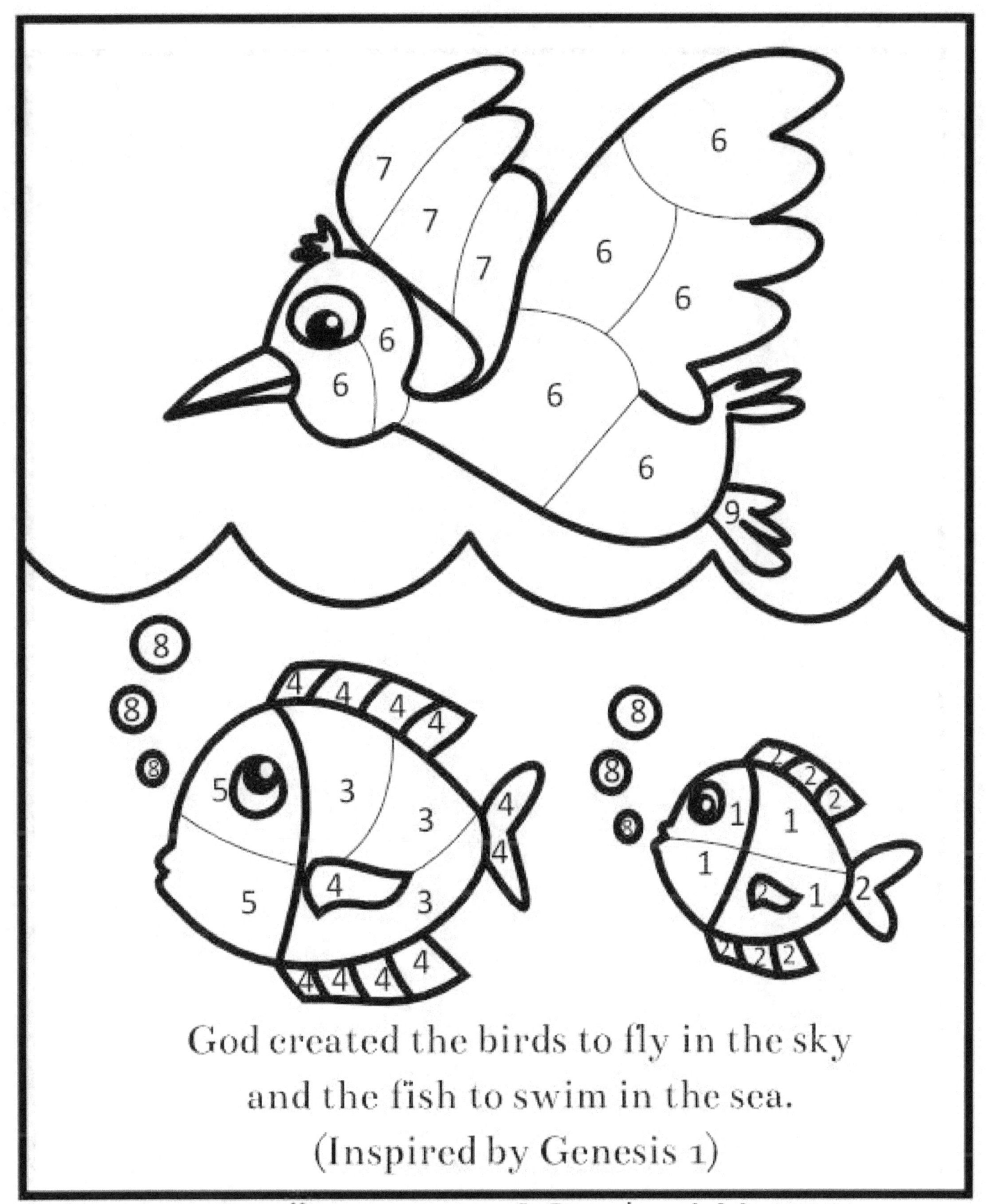

God created the birds to fly in the sky
and the fish to swim in the sea.
(Inspired by Genesis 1)

1-Orange   2-Yellow orange   3-Purple   4-Magenta
5-Light purple   6-White   7-Light gray   8-Light blue
9-Brown

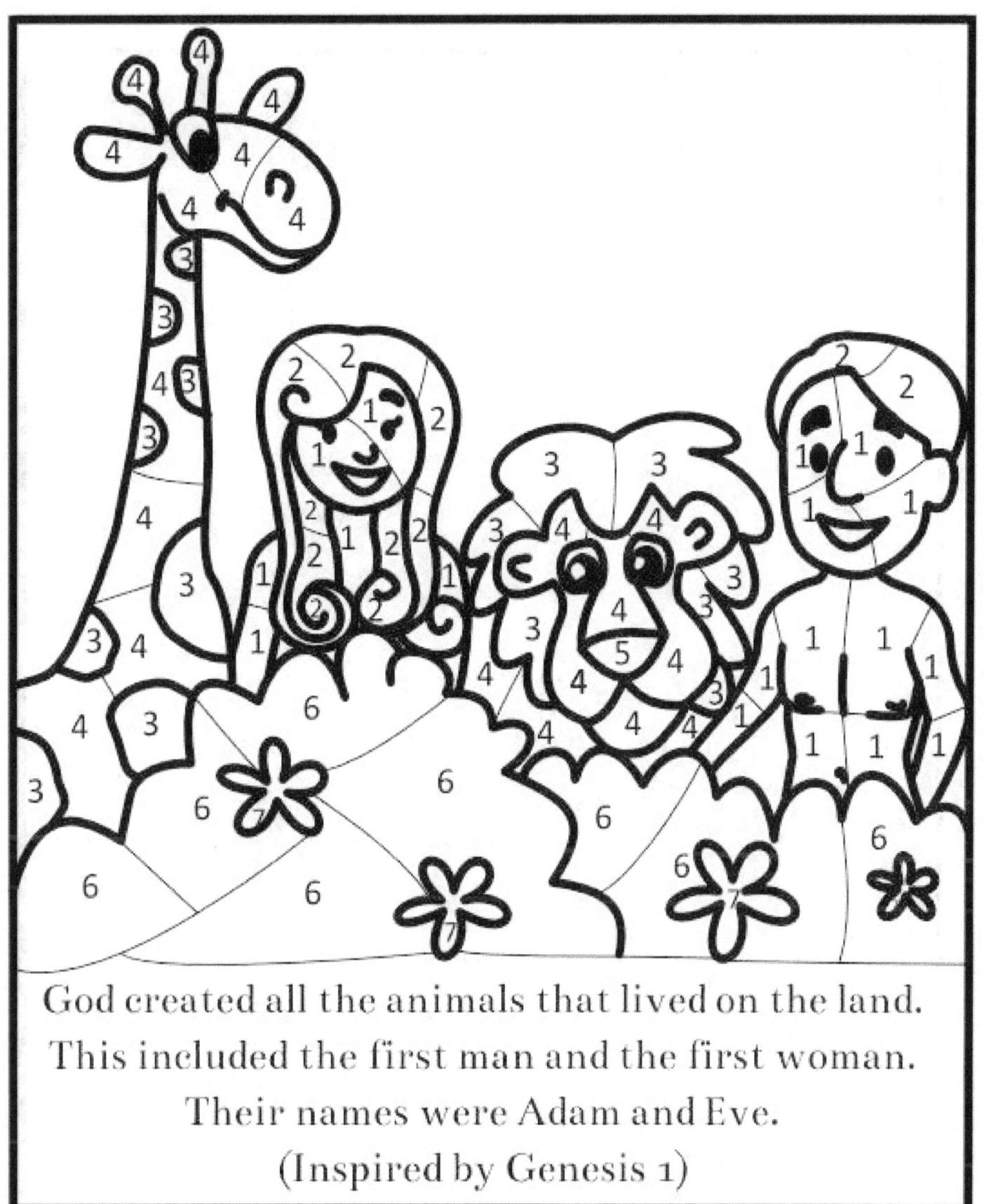

God created all the animals that lived on the land.
This included the first man and the first woman.
Their names were Adam and Eve.
(Inspired by Genesis 1)

1-Light beige   2-Black 3-Orange   4-Yellow 5-Gray
6-Green 7-Red

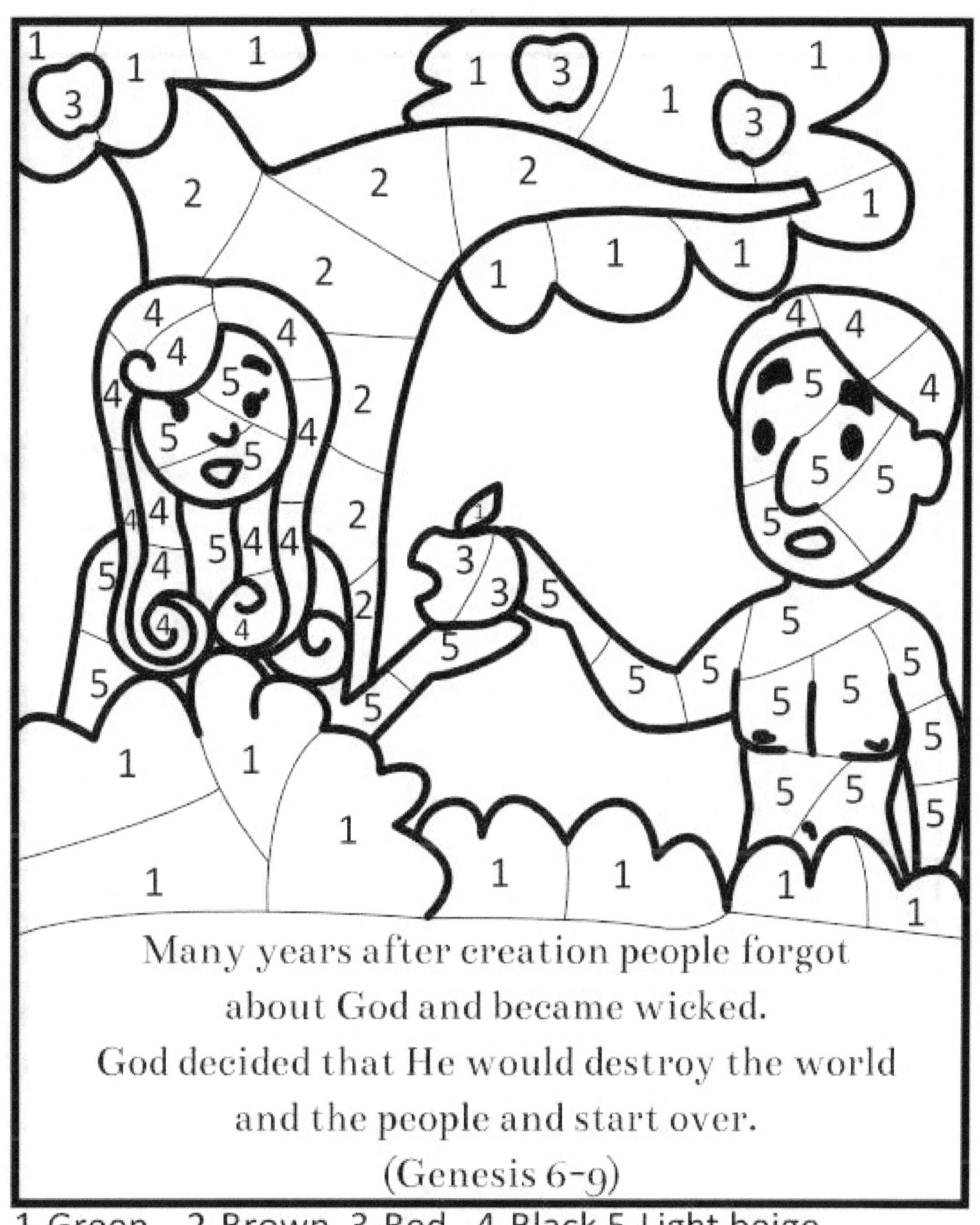

Many years after creation people forgot
about God and became wicked.
God decided that He would destroy the world
and the people and start over.
(Genesis 6-9)

1-Green   2-Brown 3-Red   4-Black 5-Light beige
6-Green 7-Red

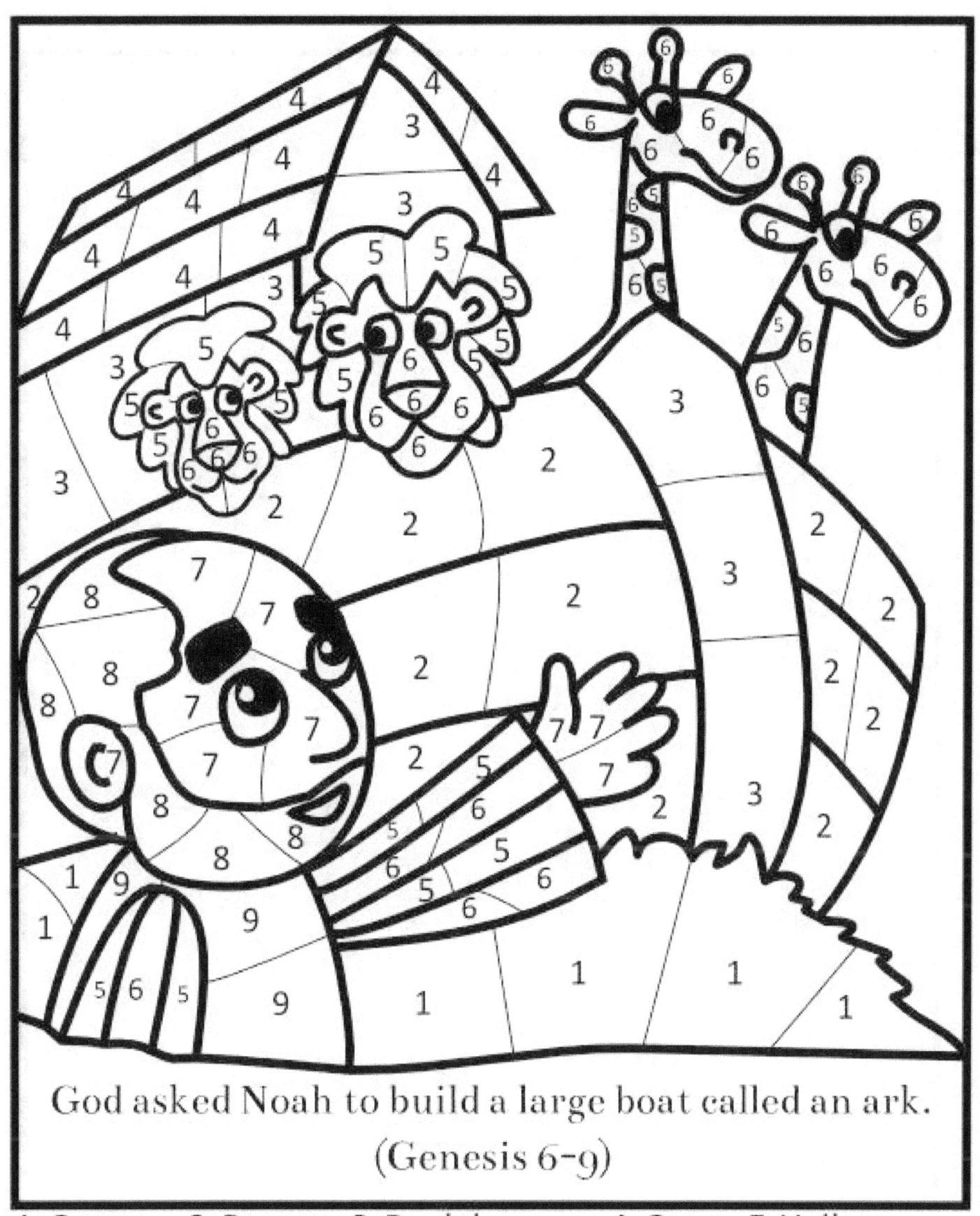

God asked Noah to build a large boat called an ark.
(Genesis 6-9)

1-Green   2-Brown   3-Dark brown   4-Gray   5-Yellow
6-Light yellow   7-Light beige   8-Black   9-Blue

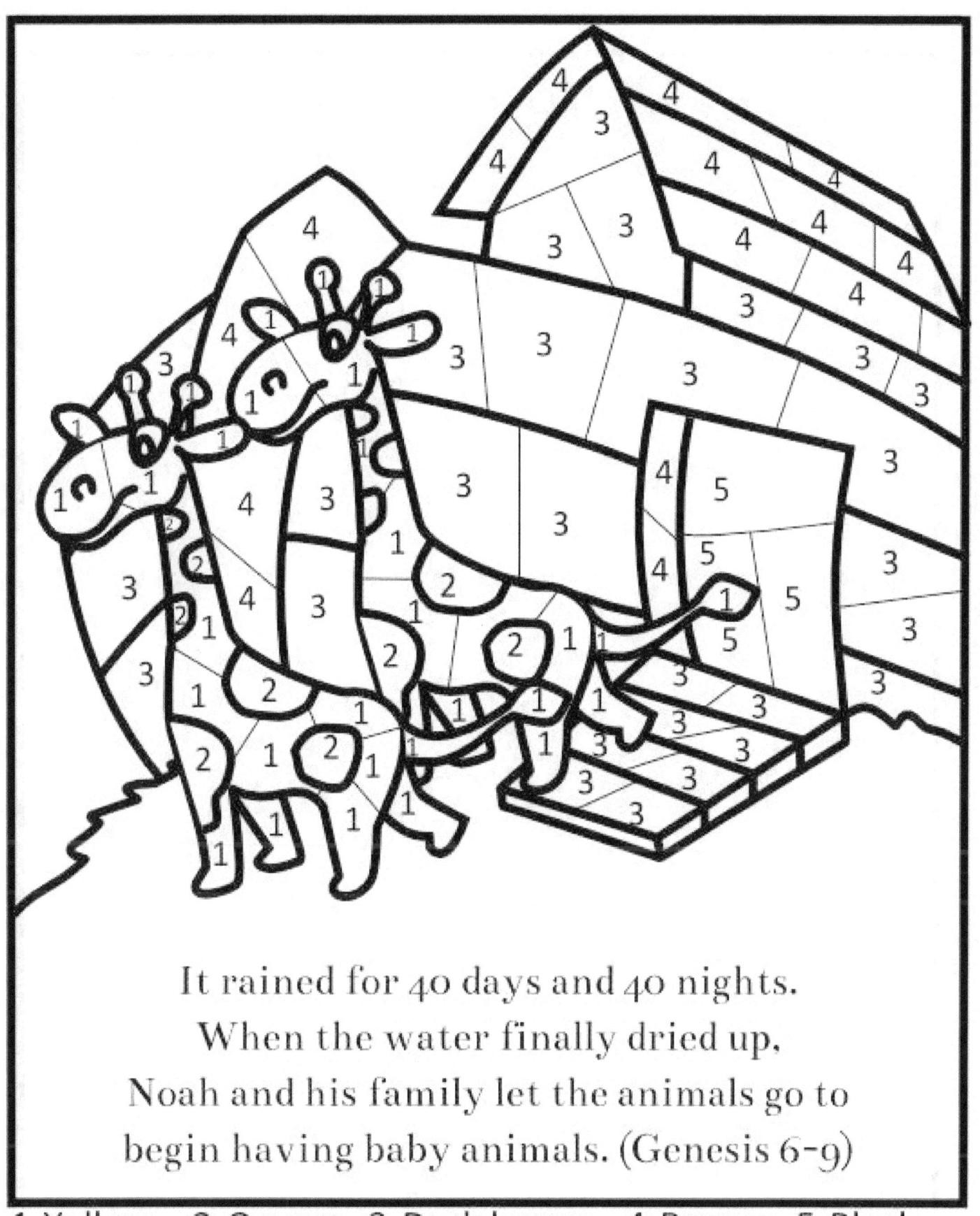

It rained for 40 days and 40 nights.
When the water finally dried up,
Noah and his family let the animals go to
begin having baby animals. (Genesis 6-9)

1-Yellow   2-Orange   3-Dark brown   4-Brown   5-Black

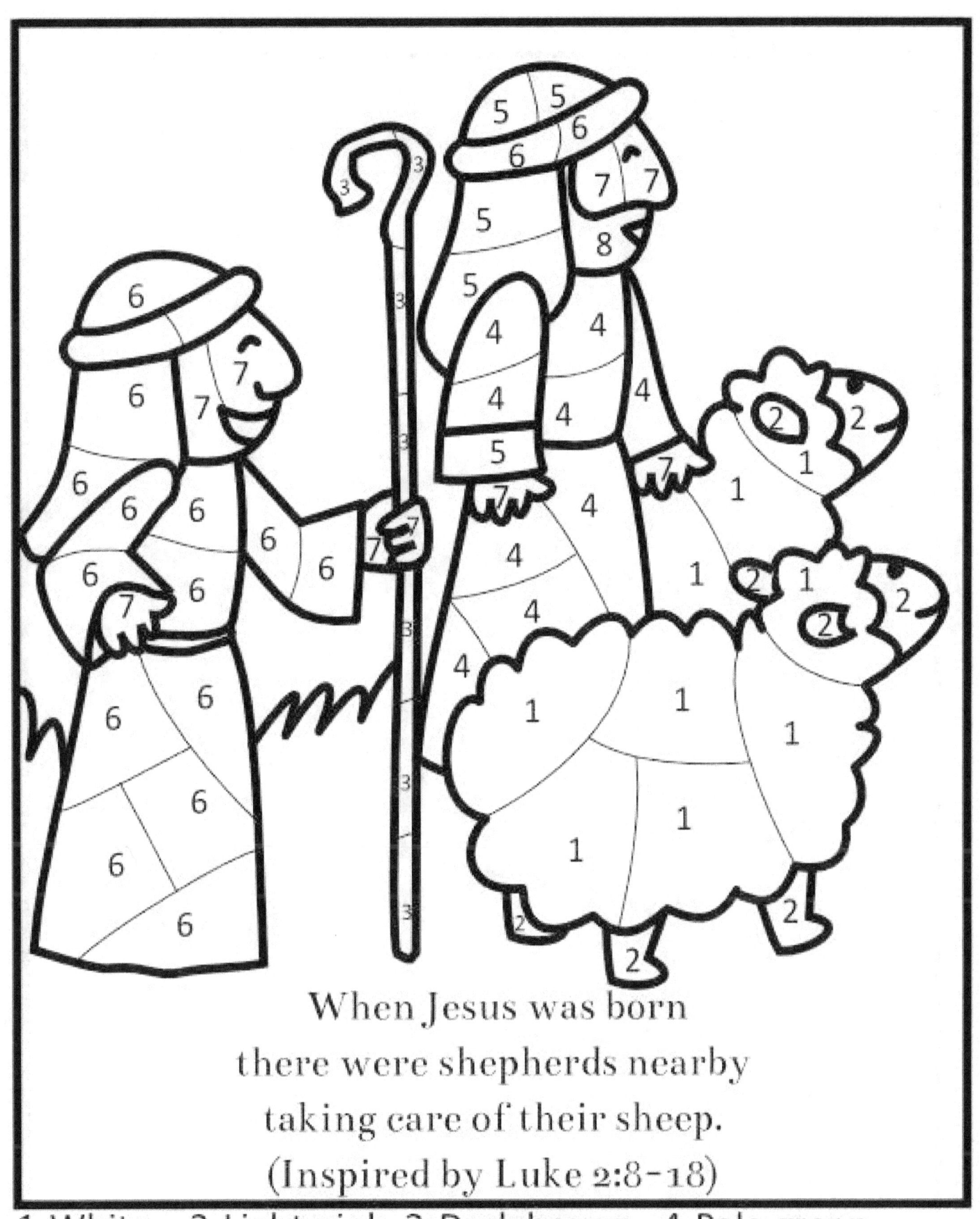

When Jesus was born
there were shepherds nearby
taking care of their sheep.
(Inspired by Luke 2:8-18)

1-White   2-Light pink 3-Dark brown   4-Pale green
5-Dark blue 6-Pale purple 7-Light beige 8-Gray

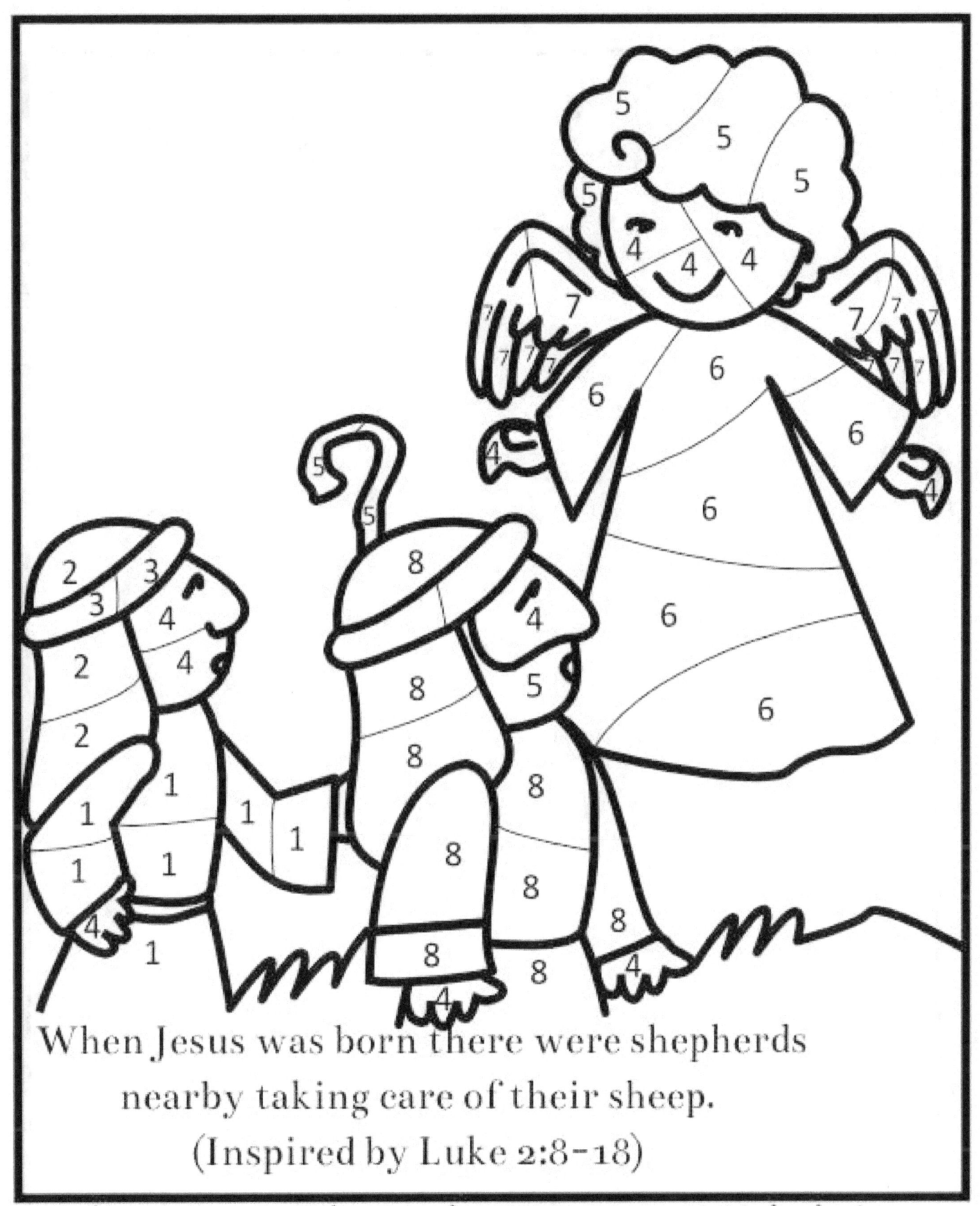

When Jesus was born there were shepherds
nearby taking care of their sheep.
(Inspired by Luke 2:8-18)

1-Pale green   2-Pale purple   3-Maroon   4-Light beige
5-Dark gray   6-White   7-Light blue   8-Light gray

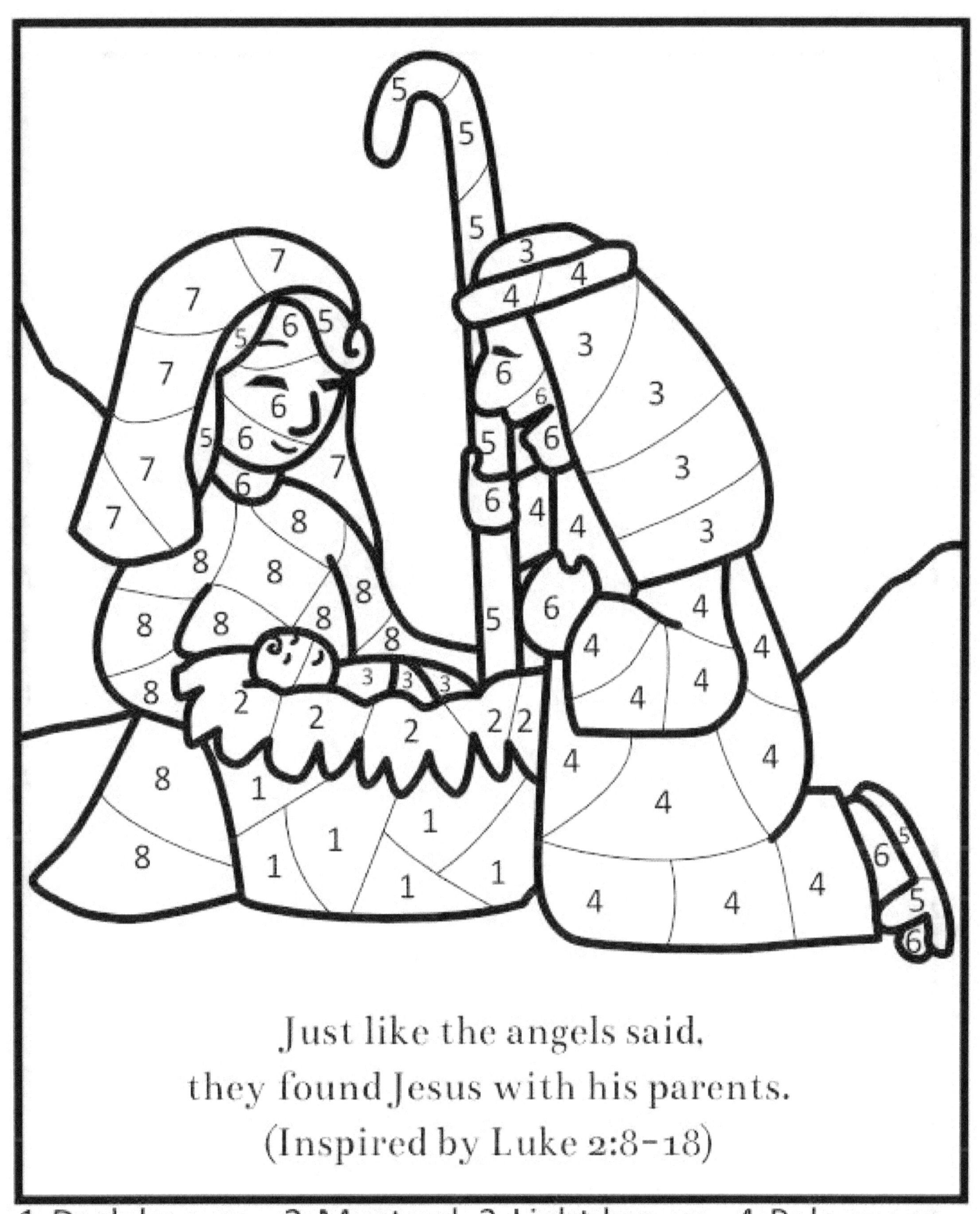

Just like the angels said,
they found Jesus with his parents.
(Inspired by Luke 2:8-18)

1-Dark brown   2-Mustard   3-Light brown   4-Pale green
5-Brown   6-Light beige   7-Light pink   8-Yellow

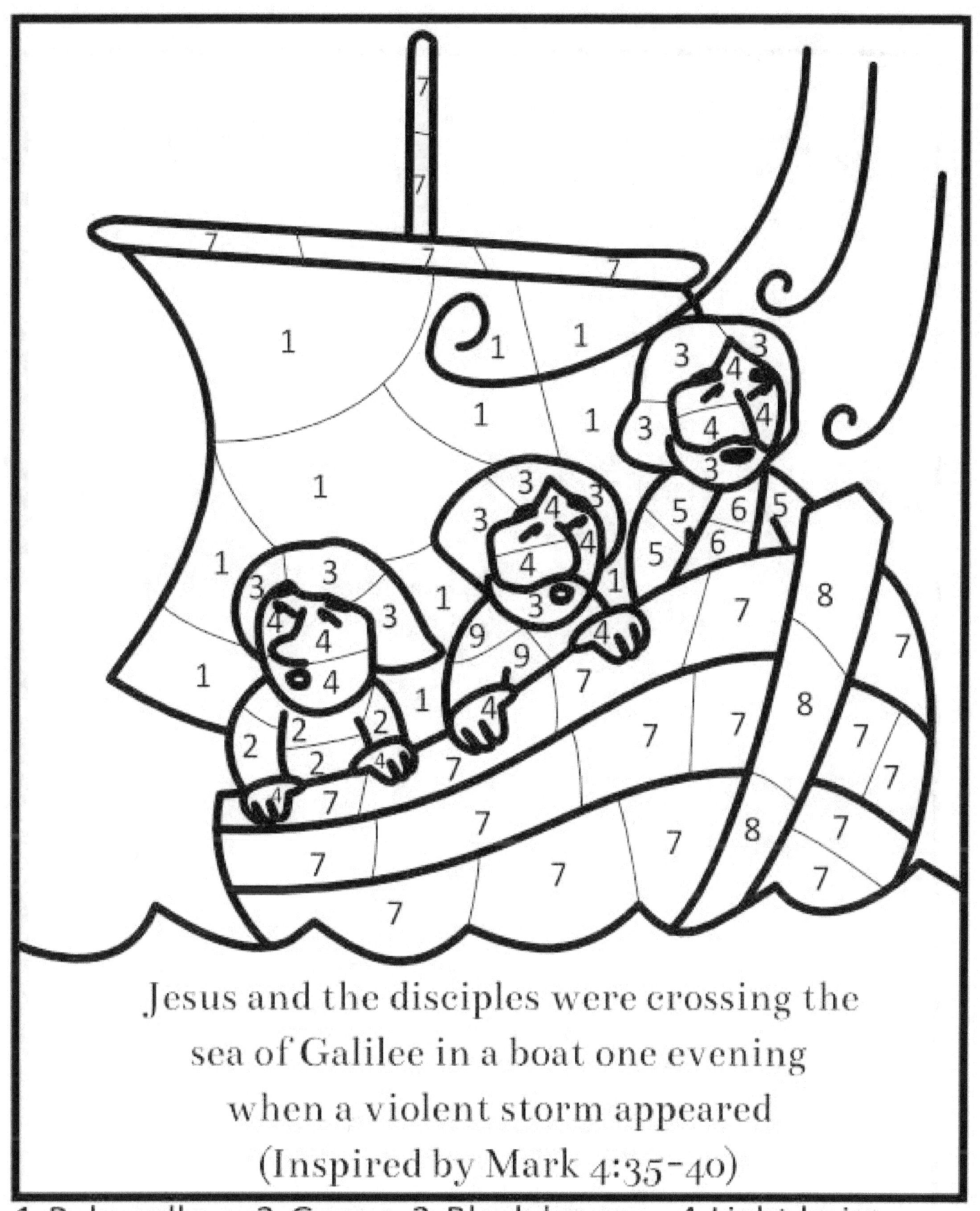

Jesus and the disciples were crossing the
sea of Galilee in a boat one evening
when a violent storm appeared
(Inspired by Mark 4:35-40)

1-Pale yellow 2-Green 3-Black brown 4-Light beige
5-White 6-Red 7-Brown 8-Dark brown 9-Violet

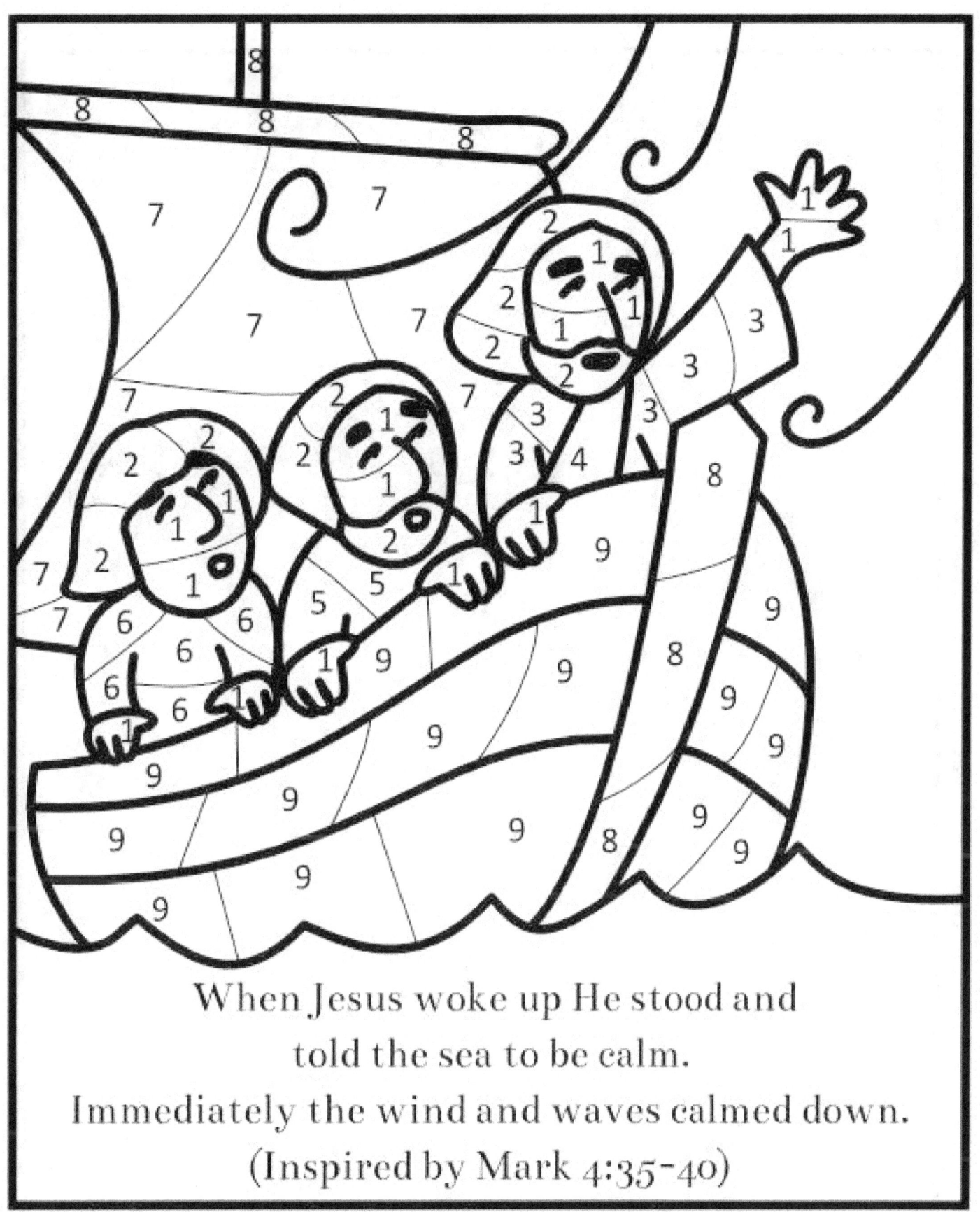

When Jesus woke up He stood and
told the sea to be calm.
Immediately the wind and waves calmed down.
(Inspired by Mark 4:35-40)

1-Light beige   2-Black   3-White   4-Red   5-Green
6-Pale yellow   7-Gray   8-Brown   9-Light brown

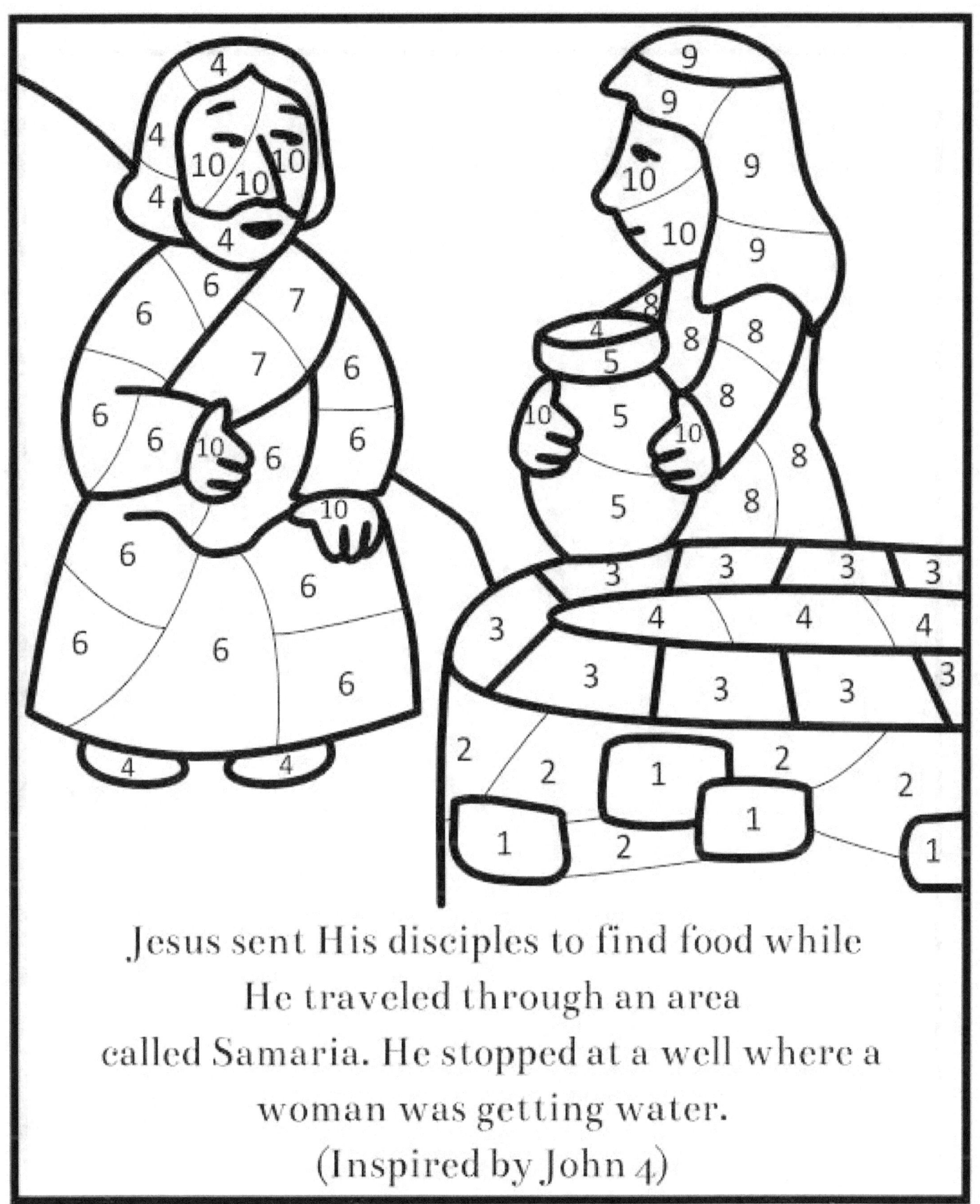

Jesus sent His disciples to find food while
He traveled through an area
called Samaria. He stopped at a well where a
woman was getting water.
(Inspired by John 4)

1-Red orange   2-Light orange   3-Orange   4- Black
5-Slate gray   6-White   7-Red   8-Baby pink   9-Purple
10-Light beige

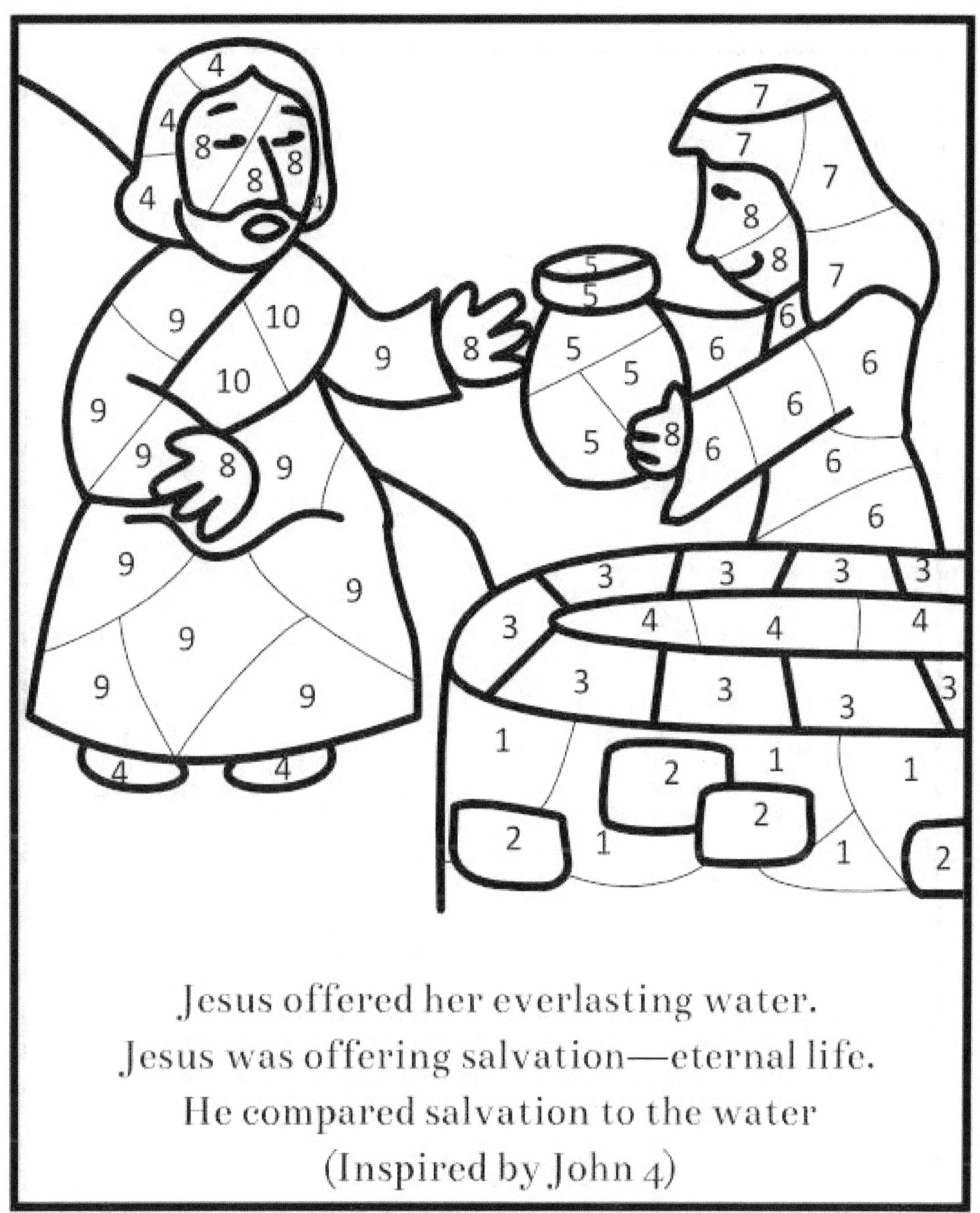

Jesus offered her everlasting water.

Jesus was offering salvation—eternal life.

He compared salvation to the water

(Inspired by John 4)

1-Red orange   2-Light orange   3-Red orange   4- Black
5-Slate gray   6-Light pink   7-Baby pink   8-Light beige
9-White   10-Red

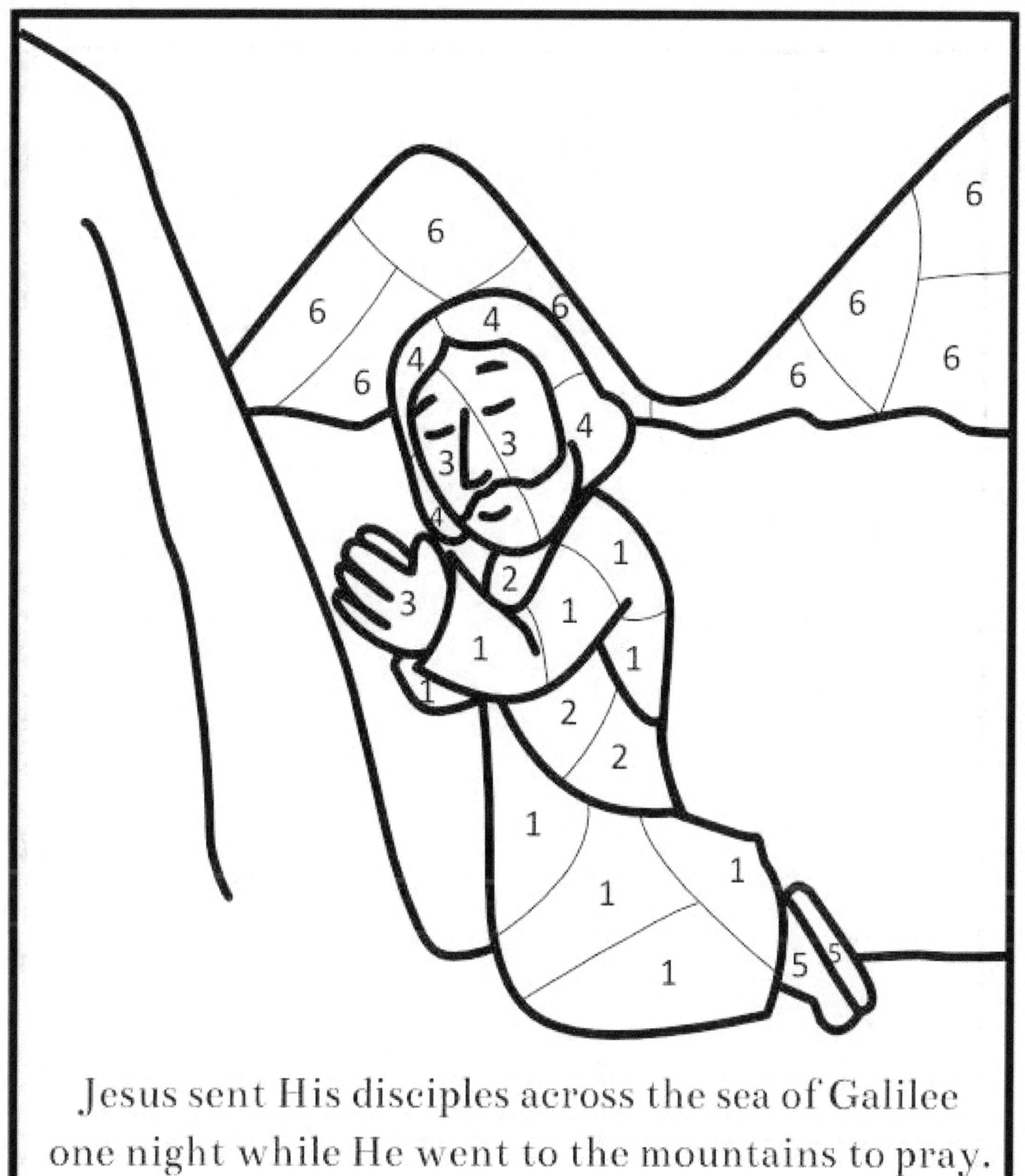

Jesus sent His disciples across the sea of Galilee one night while He went to the mountains to pray. (Inspired by Matthew 14:22-23)

1-White   2-Red   3-Light beige   4- Black
5-Slate gray   6-Brown

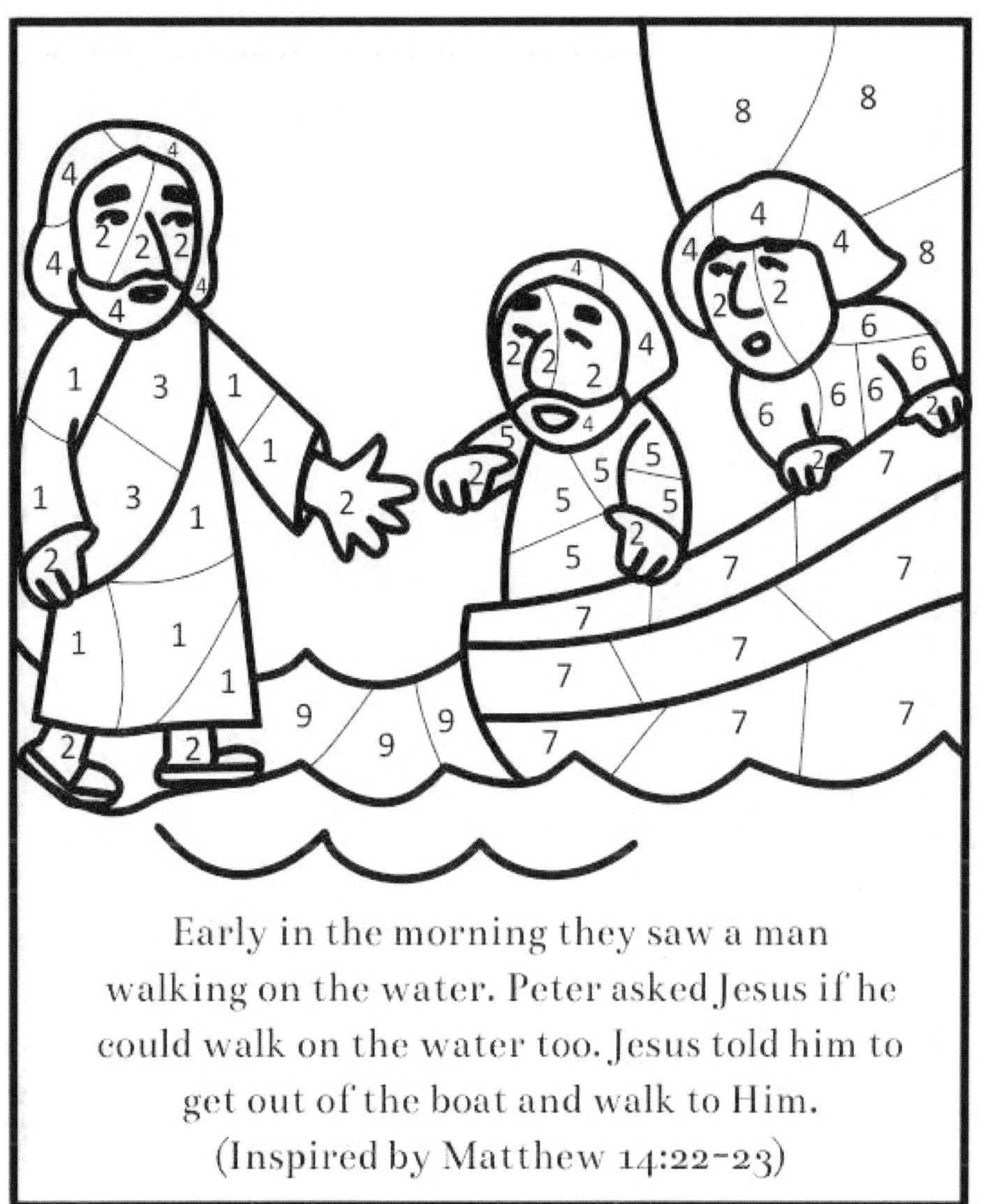

Early in the morning they saw a man
walking on the water. Peter asked Jesus if he
could walk on the water too. Jesus told him to
get out of the boat and walk to Him.
(Inspired by Matthew 14:22-23)

1-White   2-Light beige   3-Red   4- Black
5-Pale green   6-Light purple   7-Brown   8-Light Yellow
9-Blue

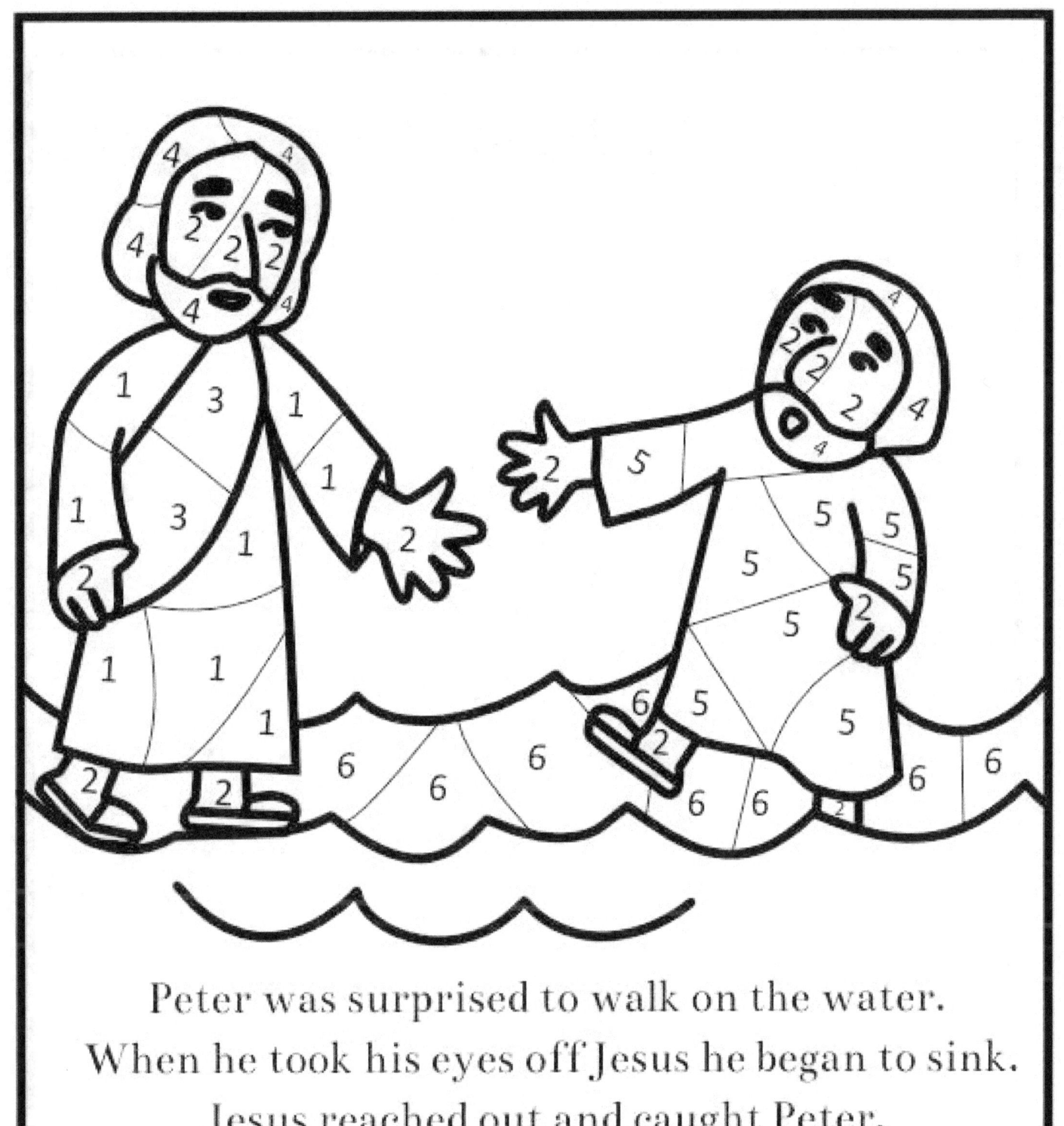

Peter was surprised to walk on the water.
When he took his eyes off Jesus he began to sink.
Jesus reached out and caught Peter.
They went together into the ship.
(Inspired by Matthew 14:22-23)

1-White 2-Light beige 3-Red 4- Black
5-Pale green 6-Blue

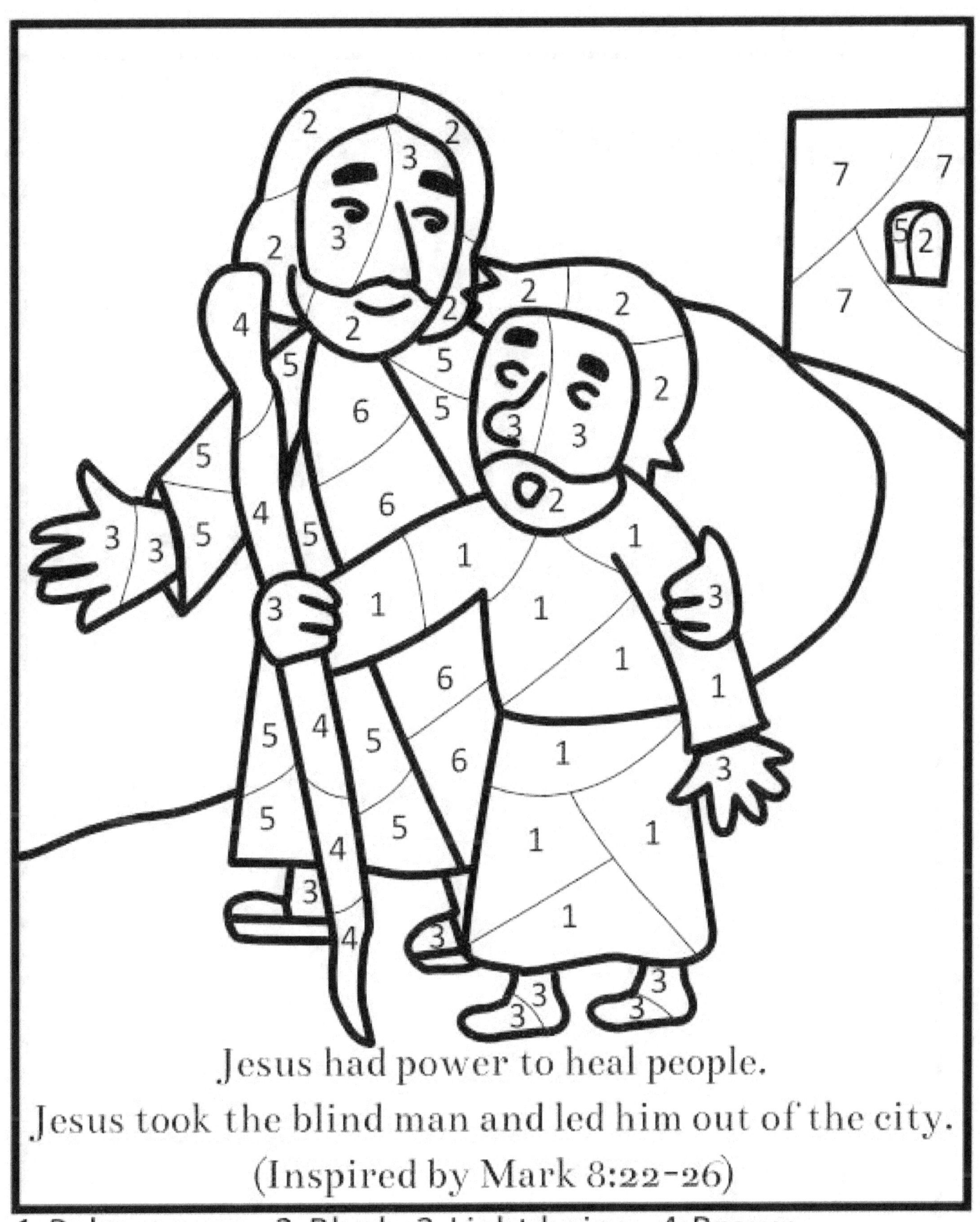

Jesus had power to heal people.

Jesus took the blind man and led him out of the city.

(Inspired by Mark 8:22-26)

1-Pale orange 2-Black 3-Light beige 4-Brown
5-White 6-Red 7-Gray

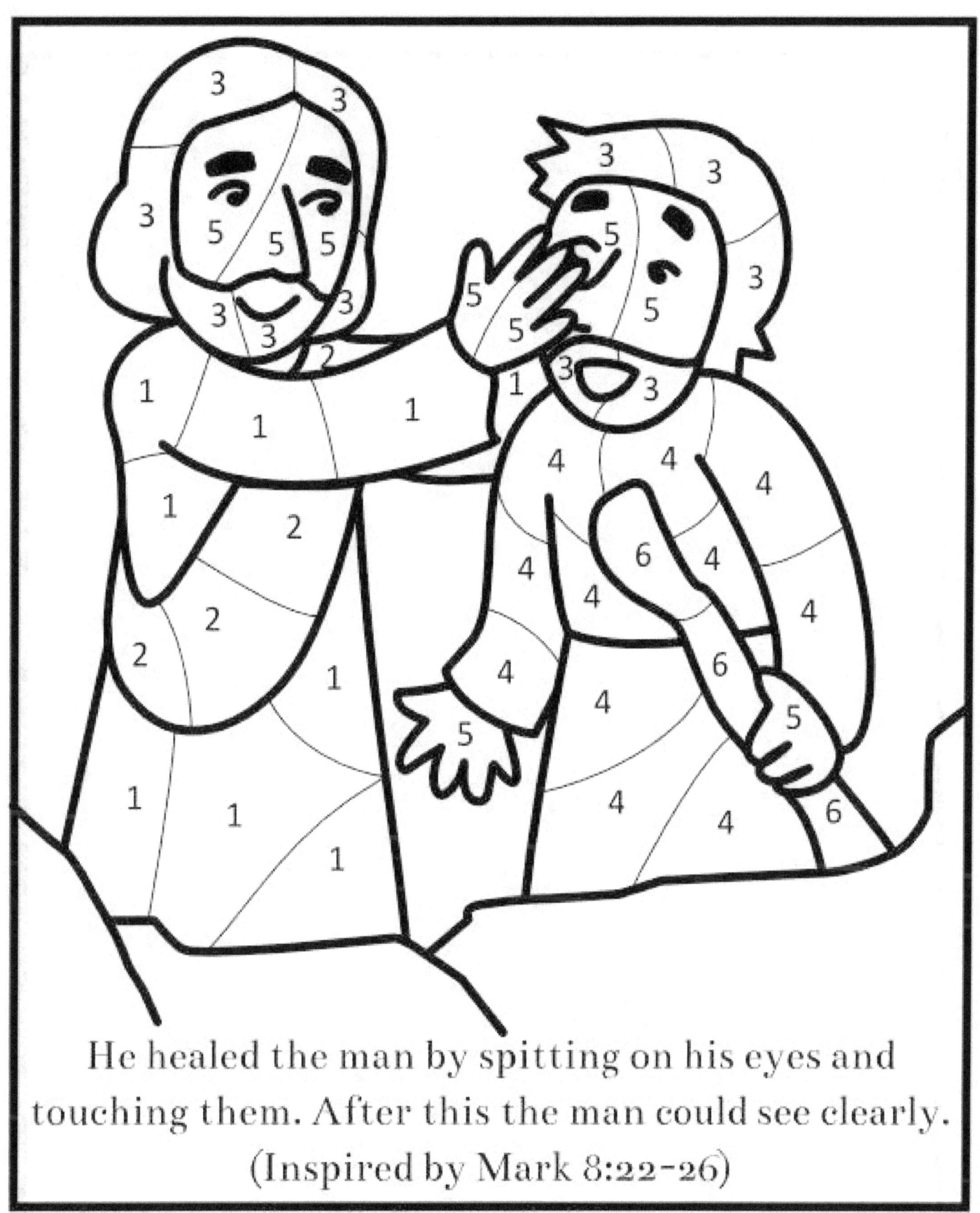

He healed the man by spitting on his eyes and touching them. After this the man could see clearly.
(Inspired by Mark 8:22-26)

1-White 2-Red 3-Black 4-Light blue
5-Light beige 6-Brown

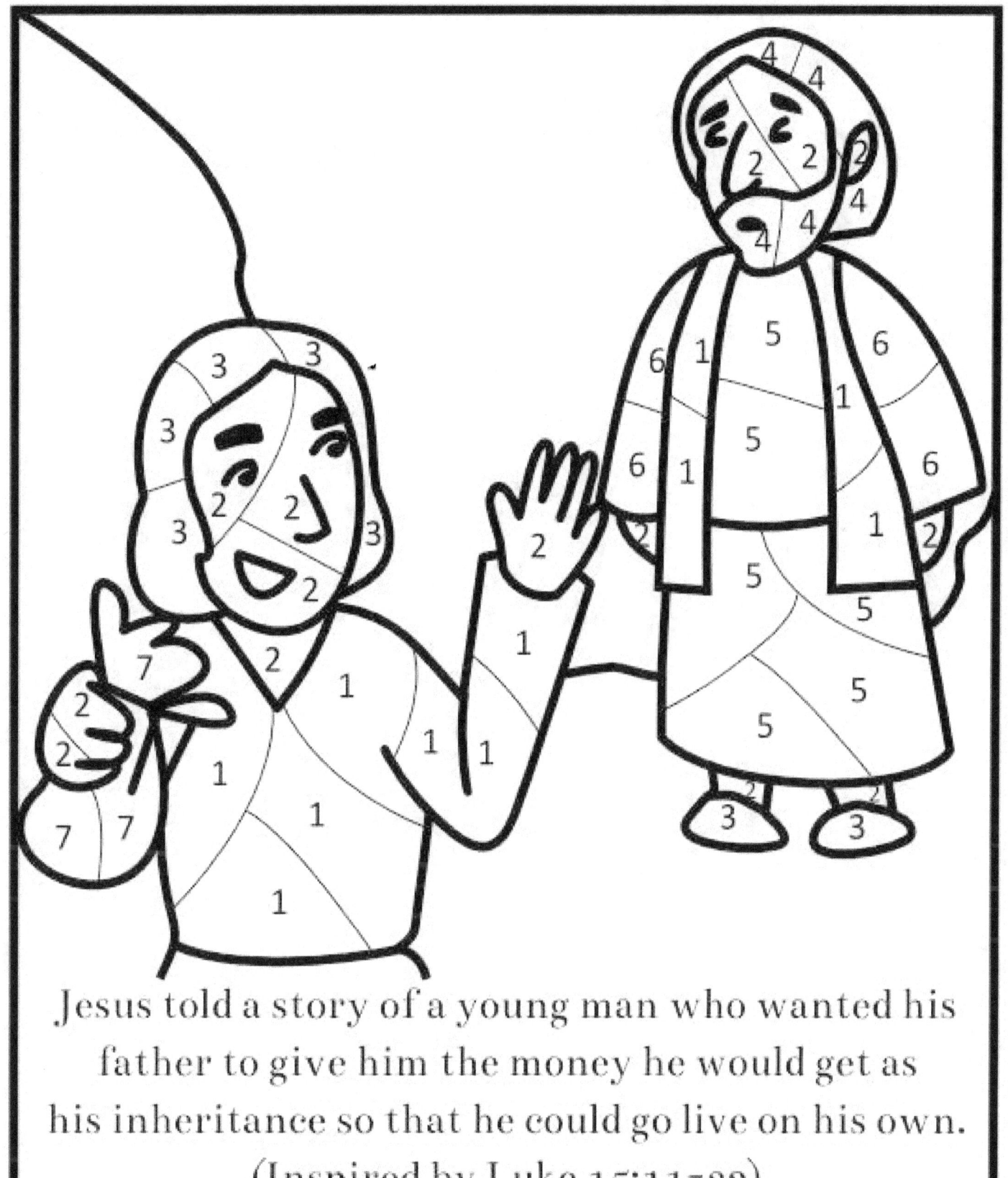

Jesus told a story of a young man who wanted his
father to give him the money he would get as
his inheritance so that he could go live on his own.

(Inspired by Luke 15:11-32)

1-Pale yellow   2-Light beige   3-Black   4-Gray   5-Maroon
6-Light maroon   7-Brown

www.ingramcontent.com/pod-product-compliance
Lightning Source LLC
Chambersburg PA
CBHW080627220526
45467CB00011B/3391

9 781710 253924